Bringing Out the Potential of Children Volume 1 Writers/Authors

Patrice Porter

Bringing Out the Potential of Children Volume 1
Writers/Authors

© Copyright 2017 Patrice Porter All rights reserved.

No part of this book may be reproduced or transmitted in any form or by any means, including but not limited to information storage and retrieval systems, electronic, mechanical, photocopy, recording, etc. without written permission from the copyright holder.

ISBN 978-1-7751178-1-0

Cover Design: Patrice Porter

DEDICATION

To my mentor and partner, Dr. Jeffrey Lant, a very gifted writer, who showed me how truly rich our language is and the power it holds, which writers can release.

Table of Contents

Introduction

Chapter 1 Of Words — pg.1

Chapter 2 Developing The Power Of Observation pg. 3

Chapter 3 Brainstorming and Getting Those Creative Juices Flowing — pg. 8

Chapter 4 Character Building — pg. 11

Conclusion — pg. 14

About the Author — pg. 17

Appendix 1 Create An EBook Today. Publish It On Amazon.com. Profit From It for The Rest Of Your Life! — pg.18

Appendix 2 Book Brain Storming Planner — pg. 64

Appendix 3 Tips & Methods Designed to Ease the Way for Writing Amazing Kindle Books — pg.100

INTRODUCTION

If you truly believe that our children are very capable learners and recognize the potential in them then this book is for you, to bring out that potential writer/author.

Patrice Porter is a mother, grandmother, a certified educational associate who works with young children and the cofounder/manager of Writers Secrets (a company dedicated to helping people master the art of writing.) She sees tremendous potential in the young and wants to unearth that potential and see the children blossom and have bright futures!

After making a very valuable connection with Dr. Jeffrey Lant, at www.writerssecrets.com , Patrice had learned so much and wanted to bring what she'd been learning to the children. Thus we have this book, a starting point.

- With this book, aspiring young writers/authors can start on the path of mastering the art of writing.
- Covered will be some of the building blocks of writing and how to get started in a fun easy fashion with the writing process.

Chapter 1: Of Words

Let's start at the beginning with words, the bases of writing.

Make it a habit to learn a word or two or three, a day and use it in every way, building your vocabulary.

For words are what give structure to our writing!

Having the words, using the words.

For WITHOUT WORDS THERE IS NO STORY, WITHOUT WORDS THERE IS NO WRITING!

Here, in this chapter, we'll evoke a love of words making the learning of words fun and part of your day to day life.

- Start with the rhyme "Learn a word a day and use it in every way". Kids love rhymes and it's a good reminder to learn those words daily, creating the first habit of a successful writer.
- Introduce your child to the dictionary with a fun game of Blind Picking of Words - DIRECTIONS - With your eyes closed flip through the pages of the dictionary and place your finger on a word. Open your eyes and see what word you're pointing at. Read the meaning and see if you can come up with a sentence that has that word in it. If you get into the spirit of the game you can expand that

sentence into a paragraph and the beginning of a story. Let the word take you how ever far it can. Some words will spark the imaginations while others may not. Play with them.

- Make your dictionary your friend, have it readily available. It's good to have it as a physical book and also to learn to use the online dictionary. A good online dictionary for kids is the Merriam-Webster Learning Dictionary at: http://learnersdictionary.com/ - referenced on the web, July 30th, 2017.
It's more than just a dictionary, they have a word of the day section, most popular words section, a place to save your words your learning, quizzes and even ask the editor. Let your kids have fun with it.

- Scrabble is a good word learning game, but let's expand it to be more than learning to spell words. Include using the words you make in a sentence. Everyone can join in to make up that sentence once the word has been played. If the kids want to make more than just a sentence with each word let it expand into a paragraph or more. We want to free the mind to let the stories flow.

Chapter 2: Developing The Power Of Observation

In the last chapter we looked at the bases of writing - words, and began to let the stories start to flow with using those words and expanding the use of words into sentences, paragraphs and always leaving the door open for it to develop into stories.

Now in this chapter we have another building block for writing - developing the power of observation. Taking in all that is around you, using all your senses (I've even included a sixth sense of the mind) to make for fuller, richer writing.

- Let's start with a little test to see where you are at with your observing. Walk into any room you know, observing, then go elsewhere. Go someplace where you can no longer see that room and try to remember all you can about it. Then go back and see how you did. Focus only on what you can remember and work on strengthening that. Once you've done some work on developing your power of observation, try again and see how much more you take in.

- I told you we want to use all of our senses to observe. A great game for that is "I Spy" but with more than your little eye. I like to do this outside sitting on the grass but it really can be done anywhere. FIRST: Close your eyes and the first sense we'll use is the sense of hearing. Be silent and really listen. What do you hear? Listen, then listen some more. You'll be surprised at what different sounds there are when you stop and take it in.

NEXT: Do the sense of touch, the texture of the grass, the warmth of the sun on your skin, the light touch of a slight breeze, you get the picture. Take it all in. REPEAT: with smell and taste. To COMPLETE the game write down all you observed using descriptive words.

- Using the sense of mind. Add to your "I spy" game, the use of imagination (part of the mind) and see what you can see in the shapes of the clouds.
- Using memory (part of the mind) go to a familiar place and see what first comes to mind, from your memory. Is it a memory of some fun times you had, a certain feeling that arises, memories of certain people who you connect with that place. This will take some time to catch those thoughts, feelings and memories as they come to mind. For more practise, encourage your children to talk about what's in their mind at different times and places. That is observing the mind, an amazing thing. It is part of our mind, our memory that is the vault of creation.

Now let's move this more into real life. If you take your child to a museum, art gallery or even the grocery store, ask questions and point out different aspects of what they are experiencing to get them to notice things that aren't really that obvious to them right away.

EXAMPLES:

1. Looking at portraits or pictures in magazines, look at the expressions. Try to guess what might have been happening when the picture was taken or what they may have been thinking.
2. Looking at paintings, are the paintings able to make things look realistic? Is this how it looks in real life? What is the difference?
3. Look at all the colors, shades of colors and use of colors in those paintings.
4. With antiques or museum pieces look at the changes in the items from the olden days to modern times. Try to imagine what it would be like to go back in time and be using those items.
5. In the grocery store, look where the products come from. Notice the difference from fresh produce and processed items, how they store them or display them.
6. Here's a good one – have your child look at

- at some packaged items and pick out which ones they like best. Ask them why they like it, what is it they like better about this item over the others. You might be surprized at how packaging and advertising effects our choices.

If you are out in Nature ask things about what you see.

- If you see two different birds asks which is bigger, ask what kind of food they may be searching for.
- Check out the different parts of flowers and imagine you are an insect, what is it that attracts you to the flowers? If you think they are beautiful, what is it that makes it beautiful? Also remember to stop and smell the roses too!
- Now let's try to describe someone. Write down everything you remember about someone you know. Each time you meet with that person try to pick out different characteristics about them to add to this list.
- Here's a good exercise to develop the sense of touch and hearing. Imagine you are totally blind (put on a blindfold). How would you find your way around? How would you fill a cup of water? How would you identify someone? Point out how your sense of touch and hearing sharpen to compensate for the loss of sight.

One last observation technique —

- Eavesdropping. As a writer you have permission to eavesdrop. This will make your conversations in your writing more like real life conversations.

Use these different games and exercises I just mentioned to develop your power of observation for it is through these observations and background context that we develop our story settings and characters, adding to the richness and fullness of your work. SPECIAL NOTE: All information is important at some time so take it all in.

In our next chapter comes the fun part of brainstorming and getting those creative juices flowing!

Chapter 3: Brainstorming and Getting The Creative Juices Flowing

"Creativity is just intelligence having fun." - **Albert Einstein**

In the last chapters we looked at some of the building blocks of writing, building our vocabulary and developing our power of observation to be able to express ourselves and have richer, fuller writing.

For this chapter we will begin to do some brainstorming and formulate some ideas for our writing projects. With brainstorming we let a flood of ideas come out, not censoring anything, just let them come out like a mighty storm!

- First brainstorming session – "What are you interested in? Brainstorm all your ideas, write them down or record them. A free recording tool for the computer is Audacity, just do a search for it and download the free version.
- Next session – What are some of the things you know a lot about or would like to know a lot about? Write them down.
- Another brainstorming session – what stories do you have to tell? Start a diary and expand it into your memoir. Yes, memoir! Start young but make it more like a record of your times. The times you are living in right now. This is great for getting into the habit of writing daily.
- Need some ideas? Check out some images on Google Images, do a search for writing prompts for kids or check out book covers.

Once you've got your list, start to go through your ideas and get rid of the ones that definitely don't appeal to you. Narrow it down to your top 2 or 3.

Take a break and mull these ideas over. Which ones seem to stick in your mind the most and that you want to expand on?

That's the one to choose but keep your list for future projects.

Time for more brainstorming. Brainstorming usually works best with two or more people working together to come up with ideas. This time were going to brainstorm for titles or headlines. REMEMBER: Write down or record absolutely every idea, no censorship. Pick out the one you like the best but keep that list of ideas for it will come in handy for other projects.

Ideas to get in the story telling mode:

- Here's a great game to get in the storytelling mood. Storytelling Cards – Make a deck of picture cards (cut them out of magazines or print them off the net) or purchase pre-made storytelling cards. - Place the deck in the center of the players with picture side down . - Each player picks out 3 cards from the deck. - One player begins by laying one of his cards down and starts the story with the ideas he gets from the picture on that card.

Ideas to get in the story telling mode:

Storytelling Cards (cont.)

- He then picks a new card to add to his hand The next player puts down what he thinks will be his best card to add to the story and continues telling the story. So it goes with each player taking turns to add their bit to the story. You can keep it going for as long as you like or until the cards run out.

- Here's a switch to get into storytelling – storytelling time can be making up stories instead of reading them. Pick a topic, the setting (use what you learned from being observant, for fuller settings), pick the characters and let the story begin.

Let's keep in mind that good readers make good writers for it is what you pick up from other good writers that will influence how you write. So Read – Read – Read and keep those brainstorms happening and your creative juices flowing!

What's coming in the next chapter is character building. Kids are usually excellent at that!

Chapter 4: Character Building

In the previous chapter we did a bunch of brainstorming to pick our topics to get started. There I mentioned how you begin your story by choosing your setting then choosing the characters.

In this chapter we're going to get into building our characters to make them come alive!

- An interesting point about kids is how they make their stuffed animals, dolls, figurines come to life in their imaginative play. The characters can speak and have roles to play. Let's build on this to see how we can develop the characters in our writing.
- Have your child pick out their favorite stuffed toy, doll, figurine and ask them to tell you about them. What kind of characteristics do they have? Ask questions like: Are they happy go lucky? Are they brave, grumpy, foolish? Ask them to describe them, listen to their ideas and make suggestions to get them into the idea of digging deeper to give depth to their characters.
- When they can bring out the basic characteristics try building a character to fit

into their story idea. Use any props you have that can help form the character and really get into it.

- Have your child take on the character and begin to have conversations making them as real as possible. Remember our eavesdropping we did to build up our power of observation? Draw on some of the styles from those conversations or scenes from movies.

- Go a bit deeper and try to imagine what they might be feeling. Put emotions into your character. This is very much how actors would prepare for their roles. A good actor really gets into their character and you should too. Make them real!

- A good exercise while your relaxing in bed or somewhere away from distractions is to bring your characters up in your imagination and just start talking to them. Really get into the conversation and let your imagination build your character. Have fun with them. They will take on a life of their own and become real. A big part of your story.

Remember to write down some notes or record what your character is like. If you rely on memory a lot will be forgotten.

This is a good point to bring up. Have notepads lying around to write down your ideas when they come. Have one in your pocket and definitely have one by your bed to catch any ideas that come when you are sleeping. Write your ideas down or record them in some way so you are not relying on your memory. This could save a lot of frustration to have something to refer back to when trying to think what that idea you had was. Remember all information can be important at some time. So get those ideas down for easy reference.

CONCLUSION

And so it begins...

We covered a lot in theses chapters. Covered some of the building blocks for good writing – words and building our vocabulary, developing the power of observation and bringing it into our writing, brainstorming to get the ideas flowing, character building to make our characters real plus fun ways to begin storytelling.

This is just a beginning to get you started on the path to becoming a good writer.

- I must mention here a pivotal part of becoming a good writer is that good writers read their work aloud to see how their writing flows. With that you get to take on the role of the reader and to see what your readers will be experiencing. It's also a fun way of sharing and great for developing language.
- When you set down to write, try to have a space that is just for your writing, with no distractions.
- Get organized so you have everything you need to write and won't have to break the flow to get an eraser, sweater or whatever. Have some files or a way to keep your work together and organized. Keep all your papers or recordings until your project is totally finished.
- There has been no mention of research (we are in the information age with everything at our fingertips. Try Wikipedia, a great tool for research.)

- We have not covered editing. Just make sure that it is done at a separate time from when you are writing. The brain functions more creatively when you let your ideas and the writing flow.
- Then there is the actual formatting of your books. I'd be glad to help you with that. My contact information is at the end of this book.

So what are you waiting for? Start now! Right this minute practise your power of observation. Right today learn some new words and start to use them.

- Brainstorm your title or headline. With that title the story begins. Keep it happening and make it a habit to do some writing every day.
- Write every day and if it is a book you are writing make a goal to finish your book and get it published. If it is articles you are writing, work towards getting them published too.

Writers don't have to work alone. Have a mentor, whether that comes in the form of book learning, a course setting or if you are lucky, an accomplished writer.

Let me introduce my mentor, Dr. Jeffrey Lant, a true master of his craft, connect with him at www.drjeffreylant.com

Connect with me, Patrice Porter at writerssecrets@xplornet.ca

I would be more than happy to work with you and help you along the path for a successful writing career.

I'm also available for speaking engagements.

Call 1 (306) 469-5741

At this point I would like to say thank you for investing in this book and your children. I really appreciate it and ask if you liked this book and found it valuable to share it with others and write a review for it up on Amazon.

ABOUT THE AUTHOR

Patrice Porter

A mother, grandmother, Certified Educational Associate with more than 10 years experience working with young children in the play and exploration program.

Patrice is a Gardening Consultant, sharing in her love of gardening and near 40 years gardening experience.

Patrice also worked together with Dr. Jeffry Lant, Internationally renowned author, communicator and educator, to bring an extraordinary writing course to the world, sharing tips, experiences, tactics, stratagems, secrets and insights it has taken a full, rich and productive lifetime to accumulate.

Patrice enjoys her peaceful life in the boreal forest but also enjoys the freedom and connectedness that has come about through her online ventures.

Truly believing in the potential of our youth, Patrice is happy to present her new series of books:
"Bringing Out The Potential of Children"
Look for them at: http://fullpotential.co.place

Appendix 1

For inspiration and to let you see all the advantages we have today for becoming a published author I've included:

"Create An EBook Today. Publish It On Amazon.com. Profit From It for The Rest Of Your Life!"

Contents

Preface / Introduction

Chapter 1 Well Begun Is Half Done
Chapter 2 Anything Goes.

Chapter 3 "It's a thousand pages, give or take a few."

Chapter 4 "Yes, look out world, here I come."

Chapter 5 Ninety five percent.

Chapter 6 Order from Writerssecrets.com NOW!

About the Author

INTRODUCTION

Thomas Dudley Cabot (1895-1995) was the first billionaire I ever met, and as I sat in the waiting room of his wrap-around glass office atop the highest edifice in Boston, his moniker splashed even higher still, I thought I'd gone to Heaven; and that wasn't a bad deduction either.

No false modesty. No deprecating remarks. No snide comments. I was deeply, seriously impressed and didn't care who knew it. I am a boy who owns it a privilege to acknowledge merit, especially when it comes packaged in billion dollar installments.

The Great Man didn't keep me waiting a minute; his handshake was brisk, eyes focused, very, very Bawston where the Dudleys speak only to Cabots and the Cabots speak only to God. "I want you to help me..." I could hardly suppress my curiosity and joy.

I shook his hand the way my God-fearing father shook hands, eyes on the subject, strong grip, no dead fish; proud, never arrogant, as good as the man I was engaging, never better, what can I do for you, sir?

"Beggar on Horseback: The Autobiography of Thomas D. Cabot" (1979).

The lessons of this stellar day began at once, and

were not one-sided. "Why do you answer your own phone?" I asked. "Because I know my business and can make a decision. You get one shot with me, and you'd better be prepared, because I'm all business."

"Why do you have such a small office?" "Because when I set out to impress someone, I want to do it with something more important than the size of my windows or how much glass they contain." I was getting a billion-dollar education delivered in the clipped Yankee idiom that screamed Mayflower, Harvard College, and Somerset Club. And this gentleman of overflowing means, no nonsense whatsoever, was asking my help because with all his ample resources and a skyscraper full of personnel, he needed it.

You see, having everything there was still one thing he craved and that was the audible, the real and substantial esteem of his fellow citizens and Earth travelers. That is to say, he craved their admiration, their deference, and their affectionate regard and respect. Without these elusive gifts from the demos, from his peers, from old friends and gouty classmates, he was merely a rich dude, and that just wasn't good enough for such a paragon.

Here entereth the cavalry which bore a distinct

resemblance to... me, a man who knew how to clear the venerable but unsung plutocrat's desk and office of their weighty cargo of unsold books, doing the necessary so they did the most good.

The man who was a notable philanthropist and fund raiser for Harvard, wheedling bucks wherever he happened to be (hence "Beggar on Horseback)." Billionaire he may have been... but I was the genie who could give him what he really wanted, a fact which became more and more obvious with every article published, for one inevitably lead on to the next until the little room in the sky had but one book left, which he autographed for me as deserved reward for a job well done, even if I do say so myself

Now I want to help you...

To celebrate over 6 decades in all aspects of publishing, I decided I would not only cut you into the secrets of publishing but actually give you a free copy of the finished product, one of the 1,000,000 free copies I have guaranteed to give away. I've made a couple of bucks over the years and can afford the gift. Just be sure to tell your friends and to study this work seriously to get the serious results you say you want.

I have lots of other free books to give away, too. Start with Chapter 6 in this book, or go to www.writerssecrets.com

Chapter 1 Well Begun Is Half Done

I didn't want to write this book. After all, I have been successfully using these techniques for years. But my friends kept pestering me to spill the beans so they could be rich, too. On this basis I created this e-book and now I have a lot more friends, rich and happy. Things might have gone on this way forever, but...

Cherchez la femme

Then I met a woman and the old saying "cherchez la femme" entered the picture. She had a web site. She needed help yesterday. Her husband had left her. She had three young children. She was just keeping her head above water... yada, yada, yada. "What's that got to do with the price of apples?" as my father might have bluntly said. "What indeed?"

However as you see, I'm a sucker for a pretty face and a sad story. This is why you see before you a proven formula that can make you over one-million dollars -- guaranteed. Read this sentence again. I am as serious as a heart-attack about this... and you'd better be, too. That means following the directions seriously. Don't even dream of responding to this epochal message unless and until you are.

Take a minute RIGHT NOW and go to www.amazon.com type in my name, Jeffrey Lant.

Then feast your eyes on the publishing equivalent of oil gushers; you know, those oil wells that just keep on pumping black gold 24 hours a day, 365 days a year. This is what e-books, properly created, properly used, can do. See for yourself.

Some of these books are as new as yesterday; some are two, three or even four decades old, proven, sure-fire money makers; some indeed having already generated over $1,000,000 each, my personal favorites. Then there are the works in progress, soon (within a month or two) to be joining the money-making repertoire. What's not to like?

A peep at yesteryear and why the vibrant future not the nostalgic past is my cuppa tea. In the older, pre-Kindle, pre-Amazon days the chances for making money in publishing were decidedly limited to a handful of writers and an even smaller handful of publishers and the media who promoted them with flagrant favoritism.

Researching the subject matter for your book was time consuming and expensive. It could and generally did take years to find what you needed and mould it into a "good read." If you were lucky you got to keep 10% of the gross; bigger sharks than you got the rest. There wasn't any point about complaining. The deck was well and truly stacked against you. Too sad.

The way we were.

It took me seven years to create my first book, "Insubstantial Pageant: Ceremony and Confusion At Queen Victoria's Court" (1979, and I had every advantage:

an ample fellowship from Harvard University, two Harvard degrees, and experts who assisted with technical advice and an ear for the occasional moments I needed to talk. Yes, seven years. Then the shocker....

Despite the fact that I got the dream publisher I wanted -- Hamish Hamilton -- when my first royalty check arrived, I was shocked, yes shocked -- by how small it was. I mean, my book had been on the front pages of virtually every newspaper in the realm, including a major story on the Associated Press international wire.

But the checks, regularly paid, didn't get any larger; that was left to my swelled head and ebullient ego. So began my search for alternatives. I was willing to try -- and to do -- just about anything. In short order this lead to the independent publishers' movement where some of the best people in the world were to be found. They were bright, fun to play with, slavishly complimentary. Remember, I had credentials up the you know what with a sunny disposition that could easily make friends and influence people.

Yes, they had everything but bucks. Attics full of unsold books; basements full of unsold books; kitchen cabinets full of unsold books. What a revolting development... There had to be a better way, and of course there was. And it came about when I did quite probably the most stupid thing of my young life. Certainly conventional opinion (re parents) thought so.

You see, I turned down a two-book contract from publishing behemoth McGraw Hill and a check for $10,000 smackers that sank with the ship. I saw the check. I drooled on the check. I hugged the check... and yet I turned down the desperately needed check, thereby promptly eliciting a chorus of blue notes of which the mildest was, "Lant, moron." But I had a hunch my future lay elsewhere... and the hunch very soon was box office.

"This book is better than sex."

I flew back to Boston from the fast-receding dreams of the Big Apple and went home to lick my wounds, applying copious quantities of liniment as I went. And then kismet in the shape of a brawny gym rat...

Instead of crying and dipping deep into demon rum, I printed up more copies of my 103-page book "The Consultant's Kit: Establishing and Operating Your Successful Consulting Business", erratically typed, with construction paper for the covers. Importantly, defiantly I also clapped a $35 price tag on it, mine all mine.

Then taking a deep breath, I reminded myself that I went into independent book writing and book publishing not to change the world, but to change my world; specifically by making big bucks ASAP. As Mae West might have said, "Goodness had nothing to do with it."

So I asked my fetching, kvetching friend if he'd like a career in publishing. "Sure," he crooned, wiping the greasy spoon vapors on his Italo six-pack. "What do I gotta do?" Just this: make me richer and richer yet. "No problemo, Doctah J."

Thus the greatest crusade in world history began. It was beautiful, a-beautiful with a slogan to die for: "This book is better than sex"; then an image of "The Consultant's Kit" rippling on a bright yellow t-shirt through Harvard Square, turning cleverness and youthful bravado into cash. I little suspected and certainly did not know I was soon to be a millionaire, but this was just around the corner. Hallelujah!

By the way that song you hear in the

is the ever-loving "Saturday Night Fever" released by the Bee Gees (1977) Is that whirring montage Travolta with moves that can scarcely be believed even if seen?

No, that wicked cool cat is me.... Lant CEO, publisher, editor, author, lecturer, promotions director, millionaire, then multi-millionaire, and now your personal publishing advisor... having the time of his life... "laughing all the way to the bank," not merely a catchy phrase, but God's honest truth. Turn the page so you can get started now...

Chapter 2 Anything Goes.

Well.... I know what you're thinking. You're champing at the bit. Yet before you commence here are some important words.

I want you to think how hard it was for Julius Caesar to produce his military memoirs, "Omnia Gallia est divisa in tres partes..." Capturing the slaves to take dictation was just the first problem. It was hard, hard, hard for Juli... on the Ides of March or any other ides.

Then think how difficult it was for brilliant Johannes Guttenberg despite his invention of movable type. Laying out just one page, one paragraph was hard, hard, hard. "Dummkopf, it's 'Deutschland uber alles', 'Ach du lieber'!"

Or what about William Randolph Hearst, the richest publisher on terra firma who had to pay for an empire of rent and salaries, thereby dramatically reducing his even still bloated profits. It was hard, hard, hard despite the fact Daddy gave him his first newspaper. . Or what about Doctor J, your faithful author and compatriot and how he started by typing his copy (aged 12 or so) on a Royal Standard upwrite and then printing it on a gelatin press, one page at a time. It was hard, hard, hard. "Mother, the gelatin has dried up, and I need 5 more pages."

Why bother? Why did so many of the world's most intelligent, shrewd and competitive people work so hard to write, to publish, and to persuade total strangers about their point of view, determined to succeed despite any, every obstacle?

The answer.

They did it to change minds, to influence, to motivate action, to enthuse, to gain adherents and followers, to make a resounding, eternal reputation for themselves... and to make MONEY as fast as they could. You see, whatever the difficulties of publishing might have been at any stage of human events, the benefits of publishing far, far outweighed them.

You, YOU, right now can do what not a single one of such great and notable worthies could do; your book going worldwide in just weeks, even days. Let's celebrate for you are about to surpass all the writers and publishers ere now... and that is magnifique indeed.

Don't you hear the thrilling music in the background? It is Angela Lansbury singing "Open A New Window" from "Mame" (1966), and she's belting it out just for you. "Open a new window/ Open a new door/ Travel a new highway/ That's never been tried before/Before you find you're a dull fellow..." If your blood isn't surging at this point, this last moment of your isolation and obscurity, not to mention cash shortfalls that rival Niagara Falls, then you need a transfusion, and you need it yesterday.

Want a worldwide reputation? Say e-book.

Want to communicate with your existing customers? Say e-book.

Want to generate new customers everywhere on our Third Rock from the Sun, effectively, inexpensively? Shout "E-book".

More money for your non-profit? You guessed it, "E-book".

I know this feeling, and it is glorious. Enjoy! Because your life will never, ever be the same! Thus, we sally forth. "For God, for England, and St. George!" So what now?

The first thing you must do is brainstorm a list of e-books you are capable of creating. This is a list you must have and maintain so long as you wish to profit (in any way) for life.

Select a major category first, like health. Or business development. Or money. Or travel. Or religion. Or education. Or... but you get the picture.

To maximize benefits, select a Big Subject, and mine it for the duration. Developing a reputation for quality content, solid, credible, understandable, and clearly written is what you must aim for. Do so and the money and all other benefits and emoluments must follow.

"Anything Goes."

In 1934 America's most sophisticated, cosmopolitan composer, Cole Porter, (1891-1964) released a tune whose title alone might be your guide in this necessary task.

"Good authors too who once knew better words/ Now only use four letter words Writing prose/

Anything goes."

Yes, anything. And that just happens to be superb news for you. We live in the Information Age and people who control access to and use of content make money beyond their dreams. Consider the following. My nephew Kyle had a hard time getting his first post-collegiate job. It was hard work, he moaned, laborious, thankless work he complained; no one appreciated the genius he so clearly saw in his looking glass each morning. Uncle Jeffrey to the rescue.

I looked through my existing repertoire on how to get your first job, how to help your boss, and how to move up to where the big bucks are waiting for you. A little snip here; a little rearranging there and before you could say "Unemployment Office", I had a marvelous and timely e-book that any exasperated parent could tattoo on the errant offspring. So much more satisfying than the vulgar and distasteful versions they so casually select for themselves nowadays.

I've been expecting you.

I was not surprised when thousands worldwide grabbed this report, the cost a few bucks; the pay-off a lifetime of income. Thus does a sensible e-book allow me to do well by doing good, just the way business should be.

Indeed I'd go even farther. I predict that sensible e-book, helping to motivate and instruct so many, will gross me a million plus over time with occasional promotion. And remember: in the e-book game a million gross is very close to a million net. You begin to see wither my Cheshire cat smile cometh.

Now let's dig further into this incredibly interesting subject, for as I see on the lady's placard in the back row, "Doctor J, you do something to me.... so do do that voo do that you do so well". With pleasure, madam, and my hat tipped (again) to tres chic Cole, who was no mean shakes about raising bucks that proved so useful in financing his ridiculously gilded life style. After all, living well is the best revenge, but of course you knew that. That's why you're here.

It is 4:27 a.m., and I am at my Command Post in the Blue Room, a place of unparalleled beauty and utility. One of its many unique features is sure to grasp your attention and imagination. Its electrical outlets are not plastic as in many offices and homes, but rather solid gold. Yes solid.

Why?

Because this is a place of destiny and such a place calls for the opulence you deserve. And so, to turn each minute of this day into specie I turn on the theme song from "King of Kings" (1961) written by that composer of brilliance Miklos Rozsa (1907-1995).

Bolstered by soaring music, I approach my desk and another installment of my earthly destiny. Yes, today will be up to my standards and soon that world will know it... and the words coming so slowly before the dawn are dancing now... yes, they are dancing. Now is the perfect time to draw exquisite truth from your brain, packaged and puissant for a world in need.

You are already on the road of giants. Here's how...

Decide how long your opus will be. 12-30 pages gives you a broad length.

Conceive a working title. You may well alter it as you go, but you need this directional signal now.

Outline the sections of your oeuvre.

Cover title and author

Inside title page including dedication (that

special person whose help was vital)

Inside author designation All Rights Reserved Year of publication Name of organization or entity publishing this e-book Table of contents

Preface. A very personal introduction by the author... you!

Introduction. Informs readers what they may expect.

Chapter 1, 2, 3 etc. Afterward

About the Author

Order form for your products and services.

Back cover with author photo and price. Make sure that photo is gorgeous, a knock-out. You're capering now on the world stage, after all.

Kick up your heels and cavort. It's a jubilant part of what we authors get, and to spare!

Chapter 3 "It's a thousand pages, give or take a few."

In 1966 the Beatles recorded Paul McCartney's latest tune "Paperback Writer." It was, I assure you, composed for me and you.

"Dear Sir or Madam, will you read my book/ It took me years to write, will you take a look?"

To ensure that your e-book is read, each section must do its part, thereby creating a unified masterpiece. To achieve this result, let's put each under a microscope, starting with length.

One reason e-books do so well is their strictly controlled length. When you're writing online (or "typewriting" as best-selling and ultra-meticulous author Truman Capote once sneered), it's easy to keep going, piling one unnecessary page on another. This tendency must be fought and rigidly controlled.

President Dwight Eisenhower, a 5-star general remember, taking orders only from my distant cousin General George C. Marshall, then finally from the President, once told his Cabinet that all memos, reports, and documents to him must be no longer than one page; failure to adhere to this strict length requirement ensured return to sender and/or the circular file. Official Washington laughed first, but Eisenhower laughed last.

If you want your e-book read and actioned, keep the length to an ultra-thin 12 pages to a chunkier 30. Less is definitely more.

Next, give yourself a working title. A title is a directional signal for you. Quo vadis? Whither your title goeth, there goeth your e-book... only you discover after a few chapters that your original title is inadequate and obsolete. Don't fret. Just invent a better, more appropriate title.

Personally, I prefer two-part titles, the first part snap, crackle, and pop (like "Cash Copy"); the second part longer and more descriptive (like "How to offer your products and services so your prospects buy them... NOW!").

Now add your name as author (what a moment!), the name of your publishing company (if you have one) and your address, e-mail address, and telephone. Be sure to include a line like this: "All rights reserved." Your book is valuable property. Make sure you protect it.

Outline the sections of your oeuvre.

Next comes the first inside page which reiterates your title and author. Be sure to add, too, your dedication. While adding a dedication is, of course, entirely your decision, there is no greater gift by any author, especially if the volume be your first. Don't forego this gracious act.

Then add your table of contents. This should make it very clear exactly what's in your book.

The next section is the Preface. This lets your readers know why you've written your book and what you'd like the reader to know what's particularly important.

The next section, the Introduction, should be brief but pointed. Reading it will make it clear to your readers why you have taken valuable time and resources. One of my professors at Harvard used to say a book should have only one point, no matter how long and detailed the work. This is where you inform your readers what that point is and commences your argument.

Chapter 1 etc.

Now it's time for the meat and potatoes, your chapters. As stated above, here is where e-books have a tremendous advantage. Short, sweet, to the point should always be your objective. Personally, I prefer 3-5 chapters of 3-5 single-spaced pages in length. You should know your subject sufficiently to achieve this goal with smoothness and clarity.

Afterword

The Introduction tells your readers what you intend to tell them with particular reference to your major point.

The chapters tell them what you want them to learn in detail.

And the Afterword tells them what you've told them. The Afterward is your last opportunity for striking home with your major point. Make it personal, personable, punchy, and persuasive.

Here is where the pen is truly mightier than the sword. Never forego this advantage.

What follows is the "About the Author" section. Make sure it includes all the relevant details about who you are and what makes you eminently qualified to write this book and address your readers. Include follow-up details here, too.

Remember, a book is what I call a sophisticated brochure. People throw away marketing materials with nonchalance, without thought. On the other hand, they may keep your e-books forever.

Consider that and make sure you have given them the necessary means to contact you.

Where is it? The Index.

There are several commercial indexing products which enable you to easily index your work. You can get them online.

Finally, it's time to add your back cover. This includes another ebullient picture of you, along with the title, subtitle, author, and follow up details.

A Note on Price.

Whether you plan to sell your e-book or give it away to grow a list and make sales is a judgement call. Both methods can work.

However, either way you must decide on a price and print it on your e-book, on the front and page covers and on the title page. Perceived value increases your response rate.

$9.99 is a good retail price. That is because Amazon.com allows author to keep 70% of prices under $9.99, while they retain 65% above $9.99. For this fee, Amazon.com gives you the world or enough of it and time to profit. And that I say is worth every penny.

Chapter 4 "Yes, look out world, here I come."

Our ancestors, particularly those of noble birth, entrepreneurial aspiration, or literary obsession, called them encriers in Paris, ink stands in London, desk stands in New York

What so ever called, they were essential in a world where communication being the more difficult was the more prized, holding as they did ink, sand, candles and their snuffers, quill pen and a knife which was constantly needed to keep the edge as lean and sharp as necessary.

Ink stands and me.

More so than perhaps anyone else on Earth, I can imagine the owners of these ink stands at their pressing labors; ecstatic, for instance, about his lordship's step up in the peerage of the Empire on which the sun never set, anxious and exigent that all the world should know; and at once, splashing ink on fine watermarked paper the symbol of his happy elevation.

Or the dutiful young lady declining marriage at her father's insistence, sobbing through a message that was hardly legible for the tears; the missive that condemned her to a 'lifetime of "might have beens" that started here with this blunt quill that was kept as a souvenir, never used again, but never forgotten.

Or the ebullient "Yes!" Master John scrawled across his acceptance letter to the 'Varsity. The Dean smiled as he perused it. It made him remember the day he opened and scrawled on his letter to Fair Harvard so many years ago. He smiled again and made a mental note that he must ask this Kindred Spirit to tea at the earliest moment.

Ink stands (or desk sets as I like to call them) were so much an essential part of life that they are easily overlooked and taken for granted. But that is wrong.

So important at important times of our life, they should hold a special place in our hearts, for they have been present at all the events that mattered, happy and bleak; joyous and unbearably painful and all the rest, every time a message must be sent; using the tools to write that message we hoped would make all the difference and come in time. And sometimes it did. "Vite! A message on the King's Service. Make way!"

Why am I telling you about ink stands? Because from this tool, authors, who remember had to make their home made ink and sharpen the quill which came from a fat goose tended by the "goose girl", who at age 5 or so was adept at shepherding her hissing charges, often with a a peacock feather. It was oh-so-picturesque... each step more tedious than the last. ("Did you forget the lamp black?") His Begging Highness.

My love affair with encriers began with a painting of HRH Prince Ernest Duke of

Saxe-Coburg-Gotha, the father-in-law of one of the greatest royal personages ever; Queen Victoria, wife of Prince Albert, the Prince Consort.

Because the Queen was besotted, obsessed with beautiful Albert, and because Albert detested the father who had hounded his adored mother to an early grave, this stunning swagger portrait hangs here in my Red Drawing Room in Cambridge rather than amidst the pomp and glory of Buckingham Palace.

Thus, there, there on the front, you see on Ernest's cluttered desk (think dozens of unpaid bills awaiting transport to his exasperated daughter-in-law) an ink stand.

Immediately you also see, and I trust understand, an error only a minor duke always obsessed with his place would make. You see, His Highness' quill is inaccurate, showing as it does the wrong feathers for a practical, actually used tool. Such pens rely on the flight feathers, not the ornamental tail feathers. But, of course, the grand ducal popinjay would want something eye-catching and ornamental, not useful. And he would get it, or else.

Custom made.

I feel I must remind you that virtually all ink stands are custom made and as such cat nip to a connoisseur like me. I have a couple of dozen, and all reflect the fastidious customer's wit, whimsy, and particular wishes. There is no "one size fits all" about these puppies. I have one, for instance, shaped like a pyramid (where the ink is stored) and features two grave robbers preparing for the grand larceny. only the Beloved of the Gods can deliver.

Then there is a lovely number, tasteful, restrained, fashioned in crystal and solid silver. It was given by Queen Victoria to her 4th daughter, Princess Louise, later Duchess of Argyll and wife of Canada's Governor General; thence (for all these items of a certain date always have a "thence" attached); thence to the Duke of Kent, the most charming of George V"s children.

Can you imagine as I can, this party boy at this ink stand ("so thoughtful of Auntie") trying, yet again, to explain to Papa King what he did in gay Paris, a mixture of boys, absinthe, cocaine, and toujour l'amour of the kinds certain to outrage and dismay His Majesty. No doubt many explanatory notes were necessary such was the riot of l'amour the Prince of Kent had always at the ready, ready to be explained away with the assistance of this tool.

You see, encriers are always there. No wonder the servants held them to the light to gain the very latest intelligence on their betters, always embarrassing... always delicious..

Probably, sadly, Greek Princess Marina, Kent's chic Duchess, may well have written letters of acknowledgement and appreciation from it when the glamorous Duke crashed while on active duty and died (1942).

I bought it from the second Duke of Kent, (born 1935) his eldest son. Perhaps he needed the money; perhaps it reminded him too much of the father he hardly knew. In any event it's here. There are no demons in it for me; just the satisfaction that always accompanies a beautiful object, a joy forever, and this encrier is surely that.

One of a kind.

I could go on and on about my encriers and encriers in general, but just one more story must suffice. To begin with, search any search engine for the film score to the 1966 movie "Khartoum". Its music by Frank Cordell is a crazy quilt of

British royal marches, regimental brass and bombast, and the strange, haunting sounds which blew over a million square miles of the Sudan; sounds that drove Her Majesty's officers and other ranks to dismay, distraction and death.

In this kingdom The Mahdi ("the Expected One") ruled, his goal a murderous theocracy, living high as only the Viceroy of God could live; the only one who understood the enigma from which everything else emerged.

General Charles George Gordon (1833-26 January, 1885), the British commander, looked for the answer to this enigma, too. But The Mahdi stepped smartly forward with the gros battalions Gordon did not have and thereby discovered that crack soldiers in overwhelming numbers explain such enigmas best of all.

Thus "The Expected One" became on 01/26/1885 "The Victorious One" and, for the moment, his vision of God provided the answer to the enigma that is eternity.

He boiled Gordon's head with its confused and muddled ponderations until the flesh was gone, and the scull shined with a luster all its own. He then turned it into perhaps the most notorious encrier ever known; an object of derision, jibes and insult. Vanitas vanitatem. There are those who may cavil with this assessment, but collectors, each one obsessed, will go to any length to secure a unique object... and there was nothing quite as unique as this... I aim to find it and again know a connoisseur's quiet, protective, secret, and profound joy.

8:01 a.m.

I have been writing some time now today, each word another thrust into the long history of encrier beauty and usefulness. "Et tu, Brute?". I should be happy. It is, after all, difficult to write when the encrier and its attendant parts constitute the cutting edge of productivity.

By contrast, the encrier's successor was the fountain pen, a nib pen that, unlike its predecessor, contains an internal reservoir of liquid ink. The pen draws ink from the reservoir through a feed to the nib and deposits it on paper via a combination of gravity and capillary action. You may well believe this to be a superior system to chasing a recalcitrant goose around the farm yard for a feather, hoping the fowl is more cooperative and less enraged than it looks.

This device first became popular in about 1850 in Birmingham, England. There are to be sure those (particularly members of the family) who believe that a Moslem brother should get the credit for first invention in the 10th century. But the case of these advocates is severely weakened by the lack of any examples whereas Birmingham offers ample evidence to prove its point.

In record speed, encriers, with their quills, knives, candles and sand became just so much ancient history, whilst every boy on Earth (including this one) became accustomed to receiving a fountain pen (in suitably elegant box) on each and every birthday, graduation, confirmation, college triumph, etc. However its hegemony did not last, and previous users were nearly unanimous in agreeing that one small bottle of "White Out" easily outdistanced fountain pens. I was lukewarm in my feelings about fountain pens, whereas my ardor for "White Out" was real, unfeigned... but short.

And so it went, from decorative encrier to practical fountain pen, to the sturdy upright typewriter, to White Out, to the self-correcting IBM Selectric II (the love of my young incarnation) It all helped make the physical drudgery of writing more bearable than it had been... it all helped us make deadlines and avoid going Postal. It was not yet good, but it was "good enough", the condition of affairs that Sir Percival Blakeney, Baronet assured us (in "The Scarlet Pimpernel", published 1905) was not good enough at all.

Thus so we made do year after year, article after article, book after book, impatiently reminding ourselves "There is nothing quite so bad as that which is good enough." However, now I cannot bear to dispense with even a single one. I even fret at who shall have them when I am buried deep on the lone prairie. You are a connoisseur like I am. You know how I feel.

And then the Game Changers that were e-mail and the Internet, arriving along with this sage book that is telling you just what you must do to make millions; a topic, an eventuality so thrilling you cannot stop hugging yourself in the shower and singing marvellously off key. You ship is coming home at last. This is bliss indeed.

10 Things you must do to produce not one e-book but dozens, bringing home the bacon with each and every one. "Hey, look me over."

It's 4:27 a.m., and grim outside. I'd rather be tousling with my bed clothes than enlightening you (hey, it is what it is), but I've got your book to complete, on time and beautifully written, and therefore up and at 'em is the order of the day. And here's the music that will get us there. It's "Hey, look me over" as sung by Lucille Ball from "Wildcat" (1960). Go to any search engine and play it now. The world is waiting to see this great e-book of yours, and here are 10 great ideas to help you create it faster, better, and something that'll make you bucks every day of your life.

1. Get organized. Stay organized. Open a folder for every chapter. Save your chapters in two ways: first by printing each chapter as written and, of course, always on your computer. Saving is vital. Don't use just one method or the other. Use both.

2. In each file keep all your notes and research data. Information to be used in Chapter 5 shouldn't be mixed with research data from Chapter 8.

3. Write when your bio rhythm is at its highest. For most people that in early to mid-morning. If you are stronger, you will produce stronger, more persuasive prose.

4. When your energy begins to wane, stop writing. The worst thing you can do is to force yourself. When it's time to stop, stop. Then work on tasks that do not require the intense concentration and focus of writing, tasks like proof reading. If you're like me you will proof read chapters three, four, or even five times to make them as smooth and accurate as possible. "Damn, how did that typo get through anyway?)

5. Data collection particularly for your next chapter should be done when your energy is not tip top. Never use prime writing time to edit, look for data, etc.

6. Set a quota. Write that quota... no matter what. I know from not just years but decades of working with aspiring writers that excuses for non-performance are legion, and you must root them out immediately and keep valiant guard against their return. If you say you will write 250 words a day, then do it... It's as simple -- or as difficult -- as that.

7. Master the Wikipedia. As far as I'm concerned one of the top five tools on the Internet is the astounding Wikipedia, which allows you to search and find up-to-date details on virtually any subject... and within seconds. I can tell you I am in "Wiki" every single day. Facts are what will give your prose heft and credibility. Wikipedia gives you the facts.

8. Keep a light, conversational touch in everything you impart. Your objective should be to make what you are teaching easy to absorb by those who are being taught.

9. If you are having trouble getting started, then write what you can in any chapter. Don't sit there grumbling and anxious that you cannot write the next line in chapter 3. Write what you can write now. You can always put them together when able.

10. Add music. When I quote a couple of lines from the Broadway musical "Wildcat" (1960), you no doubt get the message:

"Hey, look me over, lend me an ear, Fresh out of clover and mortgaged up to here I'm a little bit short of the elbow room, But let me get me some, and look out world here I come".

Good, aren't they? But then words rendered by composer Miss Peggy Lee are words that work. However even Miss Lee's sharp words are not as persuasive as they could be. For that we need music...

Now we have that music. "Hey, Look Me Over." And immediately your words are fortified to create an experience that more than touches your brain; it goes right through to your heart. You are dancing! Your office a stage from whence your message goes forth to the millions worldwide who need it.

How will you reach and motivate them? For the concise answer -- and a basket of proven methods -simply go to the next chapter!

P.S. And be SURE to attend my interactive programs at Writerssecrets.com Promotion and marketing are always at the top of the agenda, along with the friendly personal service we provide.

Chapter 5 Ninety five percent.

So far this volume has focused on developing superior copy in the form of e-books folks worldwide will want to read, retain, and read again. This is, of course, essential for developing content that people want to buy and recommend to others.

Now, however, it's time to move to the next stage in the process of generating wealth from e-books. That stage is PROMOTION.

You may have wondered why I titled this chapter "95%". That's because the business of books is divided into two parts, 5% being product conception and creation; 95% being the amount of time and effort you need to put into promotion. Yes, 95% of your efforts must be in marketing... and this means every single day. This means you. This means your product. This means now.

Helpful e-book promotion materials.

What follows now is a listing of some of the most useful and responsive e-book promotion alternatives. Treat these promotion options like gold... for they are surely that.

Note, however, that I say these are just "some" of the available tools we use and recommend at Writerssecrets.com We become aware of and add to our money-making promotion lists every day. These gems come from several sources.

Our promotional whiz Patrice Porter is on a constant, 24-hours a day search which yields a steady stream of more promotional opportunities. Let me be very frank with you....

Keeping alert to these opportunities and learning how to use them to maximum advantage takes time, lots of time, and the technical expertise to squeeze what you need from all the options. Don't try to kid yourself about all this. There is no fooling yourself in this department. When you're a member of Writerssecrets.com all this information is made constantly available and understandable. We also have our interactive programs which enable you to ask the promotional and marketing queries you need answers.

Our members.

One of the benefits of belonging to a crackerjack organization like Writerssecrets is who else is a member and their willingness to share. Here we get top ratings. Our members share. It's as simple as that.

Companies which have the ability are requested to share with us, with you. And they do. We always pass that information on to you. Just think of the ongoing advantages.

Let's get started.

What follows below are some excellent e-book promotion alternatives. Use them and profit. Again, it's simplicity itself.

1. Set up you website/blog - A word on Weebly.com. Weebly's mission is to empower people (like you) to pursue their passion. They've made it very easy to build a personal website, monetize it and easily get into e-commerce with your own online store.

2. Set up you social media platforms and interconnect them. There's lots of them so choose the ones that work for you, Facebook, Tumblr, Twitter (connect to JustReTweet.com for more action on your account), Google Plus, Instagram, Pintrest, StumbledUpon and more. Start building a following with regular quality postings and links back to your site. Facebook will let you hold an event like a book launch or special promotion and invite your friends to come. Then there is Facebook ads which are great for getting specific targeting.

3. Start your own LinkedIn group. A great way to brand yourself, and let your message or vision be known.

4.   Join groups and forums with a "pay it forward" attitude like Kboards.com, Amazon Author Discussions, Kindle Direct Publishing Community Forums. Search both LinkedIn and Facebook for Writers groups to participate in using terms like: "Indie Writers", Self-published Writers" or even "EBooks".

5.   Take advantage of a Google account which gives you an email account, YouTube account, Google Plus account, Blogger and more. Google loves having fresh content put on their sites and they reward you for it in their rankings. They'll even do some of the work for you. Do a simple Google Hangout On Air and Google loads it to your YouTube channel puts it up on Google Plus and makes it easier to share.

6.   Another big player to broadcast your message is Apple's iTunes. Set up a podcast station at apple.com/itunes/podcasts/ Take your podcasts and put them on your YouTube Channel. Add the PodPress plugin to your website, and play your podcasts right on your site.

7.   Press Releases. Talk about everything you're doing, and send out those press releases! An excellent free press release source is IBOToolbox.com. You even get credits for submitting a press release to use towards your

7. (cont.) advertising. A good paid press release service is Webwire.com. Let's not forget about our local newspapers, radio and T.V. stations.

8. Join the ranks of authors at Amazon's Author Central - AuthorCentral.Amazon.com. Create your very own author page complete with a detailed biography, blog and twitter feeds, event announcements and all your books right top and center.

9. Take advantage of the Amazon Associate program or try the Amazon Giveaway program to create a buzz and gain even more followers.

10. Get reviews. If you've truly engaged with your followers and participated in the forums and groups go ahead and ask for reviews.

11. A word on Search Engine Optimization (SEO).Using these big players like Facebook, Google and iTunes and linking back to your website boosts your ranking. Back linking to other posts on your site will help too. Use Keywords in your titles and headlines as well as in your permalinks to give a boost to your ranking in search engines.

Now it's time to join as a published author so this stream of profit-making intelligence will regularly flow towards and enrich you.

Chapter 6 Order from Writerssecrets.com NOW!

Select the package you like and start profiting online now... Go to http://writerssecrets.com

Writers Secrets Package

Writers Secrets Package

Writing secrets, tips, stratagems from Internationally Renowned Multi Award Winning Author Dr. Jeffrey Lant Volumes of his Writers Secrets series plus 35 sessions from his extraordinary writing course

From a rich, full and productive life, Dr. Lant now passes on his writing secrets giving you:

- Volume One in his "Writers Secrets" series "Writing About Famous People You Know"

- Volume Two in his "Writers Secrets" series "Writing About Famous People You Don't Know"

- Volume Three in his "Writers Secrets" series - "Writing About So Called 'Ordinary People'"

- 35 video sessions from his extra ordinary online "Writers Secrets" course.

- A copy of "Create an eBook today. Publish It On Amazon.com. Profit From It For The Rest Of Your Life."

Go NOW get the full package at: https://writerssecret.samcart.com/products/writers-secrets-package

Cash Copy isn't just a book.

It's a cash machine that will put money in your pocket
every time you use it for the rest of your life.
Welcome to **CASH COPY**
**How To Offer Your Products And Services
So Your Prospects Buy Them... NOW!**
The money-making blockbuster by America's master wordsmith
DR. JEFFREY LANT.
EVERY page of this unparalleled unique resource will produce money....
and has been doing so for tens of thousands already. CASH COPY is the real deal, and you will bless the day you got it and USED IT.

Go NOW Get your copy at:
http://www.drjeffreylant.com/cashcopy.html

"**How to make a whole lot more than $1,000,000 writing, commissioning, publishing and selling 'how to' information."**

In This Book You'll Learn How To

•	Know the market and direct your product squarely at a large and growing market that has a pain you can take away ... or an aspiration you can help them achieve.

•	Deliver useful information. Provide the exact details people need to achieve the promise of the product's title.

- Produce client-centered marketing materials. Motivating individuals to buy your product, by telling him just what he's getting, all the advantages, benefits you have for him.

- How to hammer home these benefits in an organized, efficient, relentless way that will make you money in the information business.

- Update products to sell them for years. If you've pinpointed a market in need, produce a valuable problem-solving product, and you've resolved to sell your product so long as this market has this problem, updating is inevitable.

- Creating a line of problem-solving information products. So all your eggs aren't in one basket ... or one product. Diversify and update all your products plus regularly adding new products... both ones you've created plus ones you got others to create.

"How to make a whole lot more than $1,000,000 writing, commissioning, publishing and selling 'how to' information." Over 550 pages. Only $9.95.

Available at:
https://writerssecret.samcart.com/products/make-millions-writing-publishing-and-selling-how-to-information

APPENDIX 2

To beat overwhelm I've included a copy of "The Book Brain Storming Planner" which simplifies the writing process.

BOOK BRAINSTORMING PLANNER

Are you ready to finally write that book you've been thinking about? For many coaches and service providers, a book is the ideal marketing tool. It not only perfectly positions you as the expert you are, but it also allows you to reach a much wider audience than you likely could on your own.

Think about it, just adding your book to Amazon has the potential to put your name in front of millions of new viewers each and every month. You don't have to be a marketing genius to know that those kinds of numbers can have an amazing impact on your business, with…

- Increased traffic to your website (and more opt-ins, too)
- Critical "social proof" in the form of testimonials
- Instant "expert status" (the kind that's only afforded to authors)
- New interview requests and other opportunities
- More coaching clients

And all of that before you've even sold a single copy!

Now the only problem is, well, actually writing the book.

You've thought about it, maybe jotted down some notes, perhaps you've even outlined a couple of chapters.

But then, you stalled. Overwhelm set in, or you got busy, and now your book idea is stashed away on your hard drive collecting virtual dust. Or maybe you never even got that far. Maybe you found yourself so confused about the whole process that you didn't even start.

Here's what you need to know about writing a book: it's not as difficult or overwhelming as it seems, especially if you can break it down into manageable tasks.

STEP 1: WHAT'S YOUR BOOK-WRITING GOAL?

This is the step that every new author seems to skip, and it's probably the single most important decision you need to make! Without a book-writing goal, it will be extremely difficult for you to:

- Stay focused (you'll find your content wandering off-topic or you'll feel scattered)
- Stay motivated (you'll suddenly find lots and lots of things you'd rather do than write)
- Launch with authority (no great book launch starts with a fizzle)

Your goal can be personal ("because I want to be able to say 'I wrote a book!'"), or it can be all business ("because I want to give it to my clients at my next live event").

Maybe your goal is to land on the New York Times' bestseller list. Or you might want to use it as a lead generating tool. You may even simply want to make sales.

Not sure what your goal is? Here's how you can find out:

Do a little reconnaissance work among your competitors. Who has written a book? Chances are most of them have at least a book or two for sale on Kindle, if not on other platforms.

A quick peek will tell you what the goal was when the book was written.

Does it have a link (or several) to opt-in for a free gift? Is the book part of a series of small (30 pages or less) books? Is it frequently offered for free on Kindle?

If so, chances are this book is a lead generator.

Does the book sell for a relatively high price compared to others? Is it offered in print form as well as digital? Is it traditionally published through a company such as Random House or Penguin?

Books such as these are often used to improve market reach and brand recognition.

Finally, if the book is self-published but is available in print format, it may actually be a business card, designed to be given away at events.

So what's your book-writing goal?

Exercise: Brainstorm your book-writing goal.

What is the primary purpose you have for spending the time and energy it will take to complete this project? And don't be shy. No one will see this but you, so if your goal is to make sales or land on the bestsellers' list, say so!

STEP 2: REFINE YOUR MESSAGE

Now that you know why you're writing your book, it's time to decide exactly what your book will be about.

This isn't some high-level overview where you can say something like, "I want to write a book about branding." That's too general. For this step, you want to dig deep and clearly define your book's unique message.

Ask yourself:

- Who is my ideal reader? What is her life like? Why does she need this book?
- What's my area of expertise? What do I know that few others do? What unique insight can I provide?
- What's hot right now that ties into my message? How can I incorporate current happenings in my industry with my book?
- One fantastic way to define your message and distill it down to its core elements is to write your back cover blurb. The combination of sales copy (you have to make it enticing enough to buy) with limited space forces you to include only the absolutely necessary information.

Not only that, but reading the back covers of books in your niche can give you important insight into:

- What other authors are writing about, and what their "slant" is.
- What your market finds appealing.
- Where the "holes" are in the available content.

Your back cover blurb should include who your book is for, why she needs to read it right now, and what she's going to learn. It should be no more than three or four paragraphs, and you'll probably find that's more difficult to do than you think, so take your time and write several drafts.

And remember, once you're happy with your back cover copy, keep it handy. You'll want to refer back to it if you lose focus while writing your book.

Exercise: Write the back cover blurb for your book.

What is the primary purpose you have for spending the time and energy it will take to complete this project? And don't be shy. No one will see this but you, so if your goal is to make sales or land on the bestsellers' list, say so!

Exercise: Write the back cover blurb for your book. Second version

STEP 3: YOUR STORY MATTERS

Want to know the biggest self-imposed roadblock authors face? It's that small voice in your head that says, "Who are you to think you can write a book?"

Sound familiar? We all have that voice, so it can (and should) be ignored...at least when it comes to getting the words on paper.

But that voice does bring up a great question: Who are you? And why should your ideal reader pay attention?

But here's the thing you must keep in mind: You have an important message that only you can share. We all do. It's your job as the author to uncover your unique story and write your book from that point of view.

Get this right, and you'll instantly and easily attract your perfect audience—those readers who "get" you and with whom your book will resonate. They'll become raging fans who will help spread your message far and wide.

But first you have to determine what your story is and why it matters.

Some examples of author story include:

Some examples of author story include:

- The weight-loss coach who turned her life around by losing 75 pounds and now provides encouragement and support to women who struggle with their weight.
- The business coach who struggled for years to get her own business off the ground, and who now has a unique ability to see past the roadblocks that hold her clients back.
- The small business owner who discovered a powerful marketing method that tripled her income, and who wants to help other business owners thrive.

Your story can be one of dramatic change, or an internal mindset shift, or even a very personal "why" behind your passion. Whatever it is, it's uniquely yours, and when you allow it to shine through in your book, you'll instantly set yourself apart from the competition to reach your ideal audience.

- **Exercise: Write your story.**

STEP 4: RESEARCH

Now that you know why you're writing yourAsk any top-selling author and they'll tell you that the biggest part of writing is actually reading. You simply cannot hope to write a book that will appeal to your market unless you know what they're already reading—and why.

During the research phase of your book project, you're going to look specifically for the top sellers in your niche, plus the books your direct competitors have written (even if they never sold a single copy).

You'll want to pay attention to:

- Book length—does your market prefer lengthy, in-depth books or short reads suitable for an afternoon of study?
- Writing style—casual and fun loving or suit-and-tie-wearing formal? Platform—where do your ideal readers buy their books?

Beyond the basic though, you'll also want to dig deep to determine:

- Broad topics—where does the demand meet your skill set and interest? That's the topic for your book.
- Slant—what angles have already been covered?

- The holes—this is the most important part...what's missing from the available books in your industry?

Exercise: Find and read/review at least 10 books in your niche.

TITILE	AUTHOR	NOTES

STEP 5: OUTLINE AND ORGANIZE YOUR CONTENT

There are two types of writers: those who plan and outline, and those who prefer to write "from the seat of their pants."

While the loosey-goosey approach might sound appealing, for new authors it can be a fatal mistake. Without at least a rough idea what you'll be writing about, it is easy to both lose momentum and not write anything at all, or (maybe worse) lose focus and meander through unrelated topics without a clear point.

The easiest way to avoid both of these book-killing scenarios is to outline and organize your material before you begin writing. You can do this with a number of different tools, depending on your personal preference:

- Software such as Scrivener
- Index cards or sticky notes
- A word or text document
- A physical notebook and pen

Whichever your choice of tools, it's important to outline your book so that it will make sense to your reader and so that it flows naturally from one subject to the next.

You may find as you're writing that your outline needs to be adjusted. That's perfectly fine. It's not carved in stone. But do resist the urge to expand your book beyond the boundaries of your original goal. If your reason for writing the book is as a lead generation tool, then continuing to add more and more information—no matter how good it might be—is a waste of effort. Instead, save that material for the next in the series.

An outline can help you avoid "scope creep" while at the same time answering that most difficult of questions, "What am I going to write next?"

Here's an easy way to start outlining: begin by noting all the "must have" sections:

- Introduction—if you can get a friend or colleague to write this section, do it!
- About you—why you're the perfect person to write this book
- Chapter 1—what the book is about in broad terms
- Conclusion—recap what your reader has learned and what she should do next

The chapters in between are where the meat of your content goes, and you can organize them in the way that makes the most sense for you and your readers, but do organize them. You'll be glad you did when procrastination and frustration strike.

Exercise: Outline your book.

STEP 4: GOAL-SETTING, DEADLINES & TIME MANAGEMENT FOR AUTHORS

It doesn't matter if you're writing a 20-page lead generator or a 350-page opus; the one thing you cannot afford to ignore is a writing schedule. If you think to yourself, "I'll write when I feel inspired" you will never finish your book.

Instead, take a tip from top authors and create a writing schedule. Make it goal-driven and unbreakable.

You know yourself best, so make it a point to schedule your writing time when you're feeling fresh and creative. Don't try to force yourself to write when you're tired or frustrated and all you want to do is sit down with a glass of wine and binge watch your favorite TV show. Instead, give your book the best of your creativity and energy, and you'll be much happier with the results.

Some writers find it helpful decide ahead of time how long the book will be, then break the overall length down into daily to-dos. For example, if you're planning to write 30,000 words and want to finish in a month, then you need to write 1,000 words per day. That may take one hour or it may take four, but you have to hit that daily wordcount goal if you want to finish your book on time.

Other writers prefer to set a time-based schedule, and not worry so much about exactly when the book will be finished. With this type of schedule, you would—for example— create a writing appointment with yourself every day for two hours. During those two hours all you do is write.

You may get 2,000 words on paper, or you may only get 20, it all depends on how well the words flow on any particular day. But the point is to sit down and write. Here's a secret professional writers all know: your brain will learn that when it's 10am, it's time to write, and it will naturally kick into gear at the right time. So even if it feels like a struggle at first, stick with the plan. Writing will get easier the more you do it.

Exercise: Decide on your writing schedule.

	Mon	Tues	Wed	Thurs	Fri
Word Count					
Hours					

STEP 7: DEALING WITH DISTRACTIONS, PROCRASTINATION, AND OTHER BOOK KILLERS

Along with scheduling time to write and planning out your deadlines, prolific authors know that a plan for dealing with distractions and procrastination can really help get more books published.

The fact is, life happens. Kids want your attention; the car needs a tune-up; coaching clients need emergency support. All of these things and more will eat into your writing time if you're not aware of them—and actively working to prevent it from happening.

Procrastination is even worse. When you're writing a book and feeling just a tiny bit stuck, suddenly it seems much more important that you finish your laundry, brush the dog, or redesign your website than it is to sit down and write.

And when you combine the possibility of procrastination with a few of life's little distractions...well, you can see how it might take you several years to finally get that book written.

Here's how to prevent this from happening to your authorpreneurial dreams: work out a plan ahead of time.

Now obviously you can't plan for the unexpected disasters that sometimes pop up, but you can (and should) plan ahead for things like your kids and pets and coaching clients.

- Schedule play dates during writing time to keep the kids out of the house.
- Close your office door to prevent the dog from distracting you with her unmanageable fur.
- Post your business hours on your website and let clients know you will not be responding to email or phone calls except during office hours.
- Turn off your phone, email and Skype during writing time.
- Use a software program such as Scrivener that allows you to use a full-screen, distraction-free writing environment.
- Turn off your internet access during your writing time.

Procrastination is a little tougher to deal with, because it's all on you. The key is to know what's likely to trigger procrastination, and design ways to keep yourself motivated. Some ideas include:

- Rewarding yourself with a favorite treat or trip to the spa after a week of good writing (or even a day if you're particularly prone to procrastination)

- ❏ Enlist the help of an accountability partner to keep you on track.
- Make a commitment to do something unpleasant (such as making a donation to a political candidate you don't support) if you don't reach your weekly writing goals.

Above all, beating procrastination takes practice. The more you do it successfully, the better you'll become.

Exercise: Brainstorm potential distractions and write a plan to deal with them.

Distraction	Plan

Exercise: Recognize when you're most likely to procrastinate, and decide now how you'll resist the urge.

STEP 8: CHOOSING A PUBLISHING PLATFORM

Book publishing falls into two broad categories: self-publishing and traditional publishing.

In traditional publishing, you will typically need to query an agent, and that agent will act on your behalf to sell your book to a publishing house. The publisher will then request edits, design your cover art, format and print, and distribute your book. In return, you will be paid royalties.

While traditional publishing is still considered the "gold standard" when it comes to book writing, it's a tough path to take, and extremely competitive.

Digital and on-demand publishing has made self-publishing a viable option for authors in recent years. Prior to that, if you could not land a contract from a traditional publisher and chose to self-publish, you would have to spend thousands of dollars to print your own books, and distribution (getting them on the shelves of local bookstores) was all on you.

Today, you can self-publish on dozens of platforms with just a few clicks of your mouse, and even if you want to offer printed books to your buyers, print-on-demand systems make it easy.

Thinking back to step one of this planner, what was your primary goal? Unless you listed "get on the New York Times' bestseller list" then you may want to consider selfpublishing. This option will allow you to quickly get your book launched and up for sale, and you'll get all the brand recognition and lead generation that comes along with being a published author.

But even in self-publishing, you have many options, including:

- Digital delivery, print or both?
- Kindle, SmashWords, Nook, or others?

❑ Create Space, Lulu, Blurb?

For first-time authors, those whose books are text-based, or who are creating a lead generating book, the combination of Kindle and Create Space (Amazon's print-on demand arm) is usually the best choice.

If your book is image based, such as a photography book, be sure to check out Blurb, as that is their specialty, and systems like Kindle simply aren't set up to handle image heavy books.

And again—check in with your competition. What platform are they using? Chances are, that's a great platform for you as well.

If you're publishing on Kindle (and you really should be, at a bare minimum) then pay close attention to their formatting guidelines. Because Kindle readers come in a variety of sizes, both with and without color, elements such as images, tables, footnotes and others require special formatting consideration.

You may choose to **hire someone knowledgeable about Kindle** to format your book for you, or you can use any one of a number of automated formatting services or preformatted templates, such as **Book Design Templates**.

Depending on where you publish, you may also need an ISBN. ISBN stands for International Standard Book Number, and it's a 13-digit (10 digits for books published before 1970) unique identifier assigned to each published book. Each version of a book requires a different ISBN. You cannot use the same number for a print book and the audio version. You must have two ISBNs.

Traditionally published books will have their ISBN assigned by the publishing house. Self-published authors can choose to purchase their own ISBN directly from **Bowker**, the only authorized seller of ISBNs in the U.S.

If you're publishing on Kindle, an ISBN is not required (but you can use one if you have it). Amazon will assign an ASIN (Amazon Standard Identification Number) automatically, and that is the only requirement to sell on that platform.

Other publishing platforms may offer ISBN services. For example, Amazon's **CreateSpace will provide an ISBN for you free of charge**, if you choose to publish your book with their "imprint" (publisher of record). If you wish to be listed as your book's publisher, then you will need to purchase an ISBN.

Exercise: Research and choose your publishing platform.

STEP 9: THEY WILL JUDGE YOUR BOOK BY ITS COVER

Here's an instant sales killer for books: poorly designed covers.

Your cover has to:

- Grab a reader's attention the instant they see it (so think bold colors and large fonts)
- Pique the interest of a casual browser
- Quickly explain what your book is about That's a big job for a few words and images, isn't it?

Some additional considerations include:

- Branding—be sure to use consistent colors and fonts in your cover, so you can benefit from the added exposure.
- Images—choose graphics that evoke the emotions and feelings you want your book to convey.
- Readability—when it comes to online sales, your book will likely first be seen as a tiny thumbnail, so make sure it's readable even at a small size.

Exercise: Design your book cover.

Get your colored pencils out and have some fun drawing your ideal book cover. You don't have to be an artist to know what you want, and by sketching it out ahead of time, you'll be better able to explain to your book designer what you're looking for.

STEP 9: LAUNCH PLANNING

Whew! You did it! You wrote your book!

Take time to celebrate your big win, and then you can start planning your launch.

Depending on your goal from step one, your book launch might be a simple squeeze page that you post about on Facebook from time to time, or it might be a full-blown, multi-city book tour—or anywhere in between.

No matter what your goal is, though, you do have to get the word out about your new book, and that's what any launch is ultimately about. You can create a buzz about your book in a variety of ways:

- Being a guest on podcasts or blogs in your niche
- Getting interviewed in newspapers or magazines
- Paid advertisements on social media
- Free Kindle days
- Give away a free chapter prior to launch
- Start a YouTube channel or a podcast
- Blog about it
- Share your book-writing progress on social media

- Send free review copies to colleagues/list members
- Recruit your subscribers to share about your book

Your book launch will have two distinct goals:

- Pre-release—to let everyone know about your upcoming book and to get them excited about it.
- Post-release—to make sales.

Exercise: Plan three promotional activities you'll do to build a buzz about your book prior to launch.

PROMO	PLAN

Exercise: Plan daily promotional activities for the first few weeks after release.

Day	Activity	Notes
1		
2		
3		
4		
5		
6		
7		
8		
9		

Exercise: Plan daily promotional activities for the first few weeks after release. (continued)

Day	Activity	Notes
10		
11		
12		
13		
14		
15		
16		
17		
18		

Exercise: Plan daily promotional activities for the first few weeks after release. (continued)

Day	Activity	Notes
19		
20		
21		
22		
23		
24		
25		
26		
27		

Exercise: Plan daily promotional activities for the first few weeks after release. (continued)

Day	Activity	Notes
28		
29		
30		
31		

Come join the ranks of published authors. Take the next step - Go for the **Kindle in 30 Challenge**

Now turn your book you've been writing into a Kindle book, expertly formatted, and have it published!

Start enjoying the credibility, prestige, and all-round "good feeling" being a published author!

Do it quickly and easily with all the necessary writing, publishing and marketing tools made readily available.

Are you ready to...

- FINISH writing your Kindle Book (even if you haven't started yet!)?
- Learn editing, formatting and proofing tips that will save you hours and hours of time?
- Be prepared to launch and MARKET your Kindle Book successfully?
- Have INSPIRED & successful Kindle Authors by your side FOREVER on your publishing journey?
- Get ALL your questions ANSWERED LIVE by your mentor (and mine) and expert, the Book Ninja, Kristen Joy, throughout this Challenge?

Join the **Kindle in 30 Challenge** – *Website referenced September 20, 2017. Go to: https://js241.isrefer.com/go/kin30selfstudy/Pat4u/

APPENDIX 3

10 Tips & Methods Designed to Ease the Way for Writing Amazing Kindle Books

A guide to get you out of a writing slump, to jumpstart your Kindle writing career, or to dramatically cut down on the time it takes you to produce great work. Designed to open your mind up to new ideas and ways of doing things. People will jealously wonder, "how do they get all of that done... and so *well*?!"

Here is an overview of the 10 tips and methods:

Tip & Method 1

See the end before the beginning.

Tip & Method 2

The backwards outline.

Tip & Method 3

Write a movie instead of a book.

Tip & Method 4

Take away all questions before you start.

Tip & Method 5

Change where you are.

Tip & Method 6

Know exactly what you're doing, and when.

Tip & Method 7

Reading is the answer.

Tip & Method 8

Zippy research is within reach.

Tip & Method 9

You're a character

Tip & Method 10

The formula for writing faster than you ever have before.

A little mysterious, I'll admit. These one sentence teasers were just to whet your appetite before we get to the good stuff. Remember-- this method is all about being more efficient, creating systems, and getting your mind into a better space to be as productive as possible. You'll write more and you'll write better. Much better, I'd wager, than those who find writing to be a necessary and painful chore.

That's not you anymore. You're a happily efficient writer with the potential to start making some money writing.

Tip & Method 1

See the end before the beginning.

You've been told to create outlines before you get started writing. You've been told that this takes away writer's block and gives you a smooth path as you write. All of that is true...there's just one problem. Your writer's block and uncertainty can be so severe that you can't even get that far. What do you do then? If you're like most writers, you sit around feeling anxious with your fingers motionlessly poised over the keyboard. You waste minutes, if not hours, with this uncertainty. It zaps your creativity and your best ideas.

This problem (I think we all go through it) got me thinking about what I know about success. Masters of productivity and goal setting tell us to create vision boards, mind movies, and things like that to become more successful. We're supposed to use these visuals to motivate ourselves to drop the weight, boost our incomes, or whatever will lead us to our goal.

The more I thought about it, the more I realized the same thing can apply to writing a book. We

Tip & Method 1 (cont.)

can think about the smaller pieces (the outline) all we want. But it doesn't *mean* anything unless we know what the result will be. Where is the story going? What is the point?

We know that we can be more successful if we have a vision in mind of what success looks like. By the same token, we can be more successful if we have a vision of what our book looks like. What's the ending? What's the purpose?

I've written about this quite a bit recently, and I call it "visualizing Point B". In other words, if you have a destination in mind, whether a trip, a goal, or in this case a completed book, before you start on your journey, you need to know where you're going... getting from Point A (where you are now) to Point B (where you want to end up).

Now, I want you to think about the book you need to write.

If fiction: Set a timer for 10 minutes and brainstorm your ending. Where will your

Tip & Method 1 (cont.)

characters be by the end? You may know how the book will start or who will be in it, but how will it end? Have fun as you brainstorm. No idea is too crazy.

Then, go through and choose the ideal ending from what you've brainstormed-- choose the one that stands out to you the most.

The pieces of your outline should now fall into place when you go to create the rest of the outline and start to write. You know where you're going, so it's much easier to map your course for getting there.

If nonfiction: The process is a bit different with non-fiction, of course, because you're not really coming up with an ending. In a non-fiction book, the ending generally summarizes everything the book contained. You try to inspire people and get them thinking, caught up in what they've just learned or felt.

Go ahead and write that ending section now (it only has to be a few paragraphs for this exercise)

Tip & Method 1 (cont.)

You have your ending, so now you can easily work toward it-- it's a more freeing way of outlining. Sure, you may not know everything that will go into your book yet and you may never actually use this "ending." But, it will relieve your mind of the duty of thinking as you write, leaving room for creativity and solid writing.

This is a mind trick as much as an organizational trick. We all want to get to the end, right? Writers don't like to write; they like to have written (a spin-off of Michael Kanin's, "I don't like to write, but I love to have written"). Well, you're at the end already. Your mind is at ease and you're ready to put the rest of the pieces in place.

This isn't to say that you can never change your ending. Your story will tell you where to go. The point is that you now have direction and you don't have to think about it. You can be as creative and free because the pressure of "the perfect ending" is gone.

Tip & Method 2

The backwards outline.

You have the end in mind after cheat #1. You know how to create a traditional outline. Now I want you to try something that isn't as traditional-- create a backwards outline.

Outlines usually consist of major talking points and sub points. That's a great method and works very well for a lot of people. But outlines sometimes become too focused on "me, me, me" the author, instead of on the readers.

Great writers are supposed to pay attention to their audience. They are supposed to be able to reach their audience on an emotional level, delivering on the very thing the reader hoped to gain from reading the book, and more.

Too many writers get bogged down on the mechanics of the outline instead of on the expected outcome of the outline. I hope that makes sense. Emotions, feelings, and the power of words get lost in the mechanics of writing and outlining.

Tip & Method 2 (cont.)

Let's take a different approach. This approach gets the very best writing out of you while also giving the very best to your reader. Best of all, this method will help you write more quickly and become more excited about your writing.

This exercise is all about emotions and feelings. Go ahead and get a general idea of what each chapter will be about. For fiction, which scenes will each chapter contain? For non-fiction, what information will be in each chapter? This should be a very rough, quick outline with few details-- there is plenty of time to fill that out later.

Now that you have your list of chapters and a general idea of what they will contain, it's time to think about the result of those chapters. When the book is written, what will the reader feel or think after reading chapter one? How about chapter two? Chapter 3? Go through each chapter in turn and use this method of backwards outlining. It's "backwards" because you're thinking about desired results and feelings instead of facts, figures, and structure.

Tip & Method 2 (cont.)

Here is a fiction example:

Chapter One

General idea: *Princess hates her posh life and wants to escape from the castle.*

Reader should feel: *Skeptical about this spoiled girl, yet intrigued at the same time because they see a little of themselves in her desire for something more.*

Do you see how easy it will now be to fill out the rest of the outline for chapter one? You've started with your desired result, which got your brain working with possibilities. Now will take just a few minutes to sketch the details for chapter one. You may have just stared at your outline, baffled, for hours before this trick.

Here is a non-fiction example:

General idea: *Writing great books for Kindle is actually easier than most people think.*

Tip & Method 2
Non-fiction example (cont.)

Reader should feel: Like I understand them. They should feel hope and excitement about learning new methods to write faster and better. Possibly skeptical and unsure, but anxious and excited to move past the first chapter.

Did I capture some of what you felt as you read the first chapter? I hope so-- it helped me figure out what to write and which emotional hot points to hit on. It then became very easy to write the introduction.

Do this with each chapter you're going to write and the book will practically write itself... Partially because you've hyper focused on the reader. Everything comes into focus when you do that. It's so much easier to write and to feel excited about your writing when you do this. No more writer's block and no more hesitation to sit down and write-- I dare say, this method makes it fun to write.

Tip & Method 3
Write a movie instead of a book.

No, I'm not saying you should get out there and write a screenplay. I'm saying you should feel and know your characters as deeply as you would if you were directing them in a movie. You should know what they look like, what their background is, what their physical and emotional flaws are, and more.

Many writers struggle to get to know their characters. They get frustrated and experience writer's block because they don't have a clear enough picture of who their characters are. It's one thing to "direct" people you can see and hear. It's another to try to "direct" characters who don't yet exist and haven't come alive in your mind.

You need to make your characters live before you get started writing so they are easier to direct. If they are alive, it's much easier to take them in unexpected and magical places because you don't have to spend any energy wondering who they are.

Tip & Method 3 (cont.)

How do you do this?

You create them.

Flip through a magazine and find people who represent each character. Find and cut out objects, travel destinations, homes, and other photos and graphics that represent who your character is and what they love, hate, do, and feel. Paste your character and the other images to a poster board so you can glance up and see your character whenever you need to. Do this for each major character and you'll be surrounded by "people" who have actual lives instead of a few lines of flat, typed characteristics. Alternatively, create this "poster" on your computer using digital images for easy access.

It will be so much easier to write compelling scenes, dialogue, and descriptions once you do this. Make your characters live and you'll write more quickly, write better, and write more productively. Have fun with this-- it sincerely will banish writer's block and anxiety in writing fiction.

Tip & Method 4

Take away all questions before you start.

Some writers try to write with only a vague notion of what they are going to write about. That can work for some writers, but you might not be one of them if you struggle with writer's block, inconsistency, plot holes, and a number of other issues that will sink your Kindle book.

Many writers "interview" their characters before they sit down to write. They pretend to have their characters tell them about their lives, past, present, and future. This is a really great technique, but let's take it a step further. You are going to ask your characters how they feel about everything that happens in the story.

At this point, you likely have your major plot points figured out. But, every writer has experienced the frustration that comes along when they just don't know how to move the plot forward or how to solve a plot hole that doesn't make sense. Stewing about these problems can put a giant kink in the works. It's almost impossible to move forward if these questions are hovering over you, unanswered.

Tip & Method 4
Take away all questions before you start.

Some writers try to write with only a vague notion of what they are going to write about. That can work for some writers, but you might not be one of them if you struggle with writer's block, inconsistency, plot holes, and a number of other issues that will sink your Kindle book.

Many writers "interview" their characters before they sit down to write. They pretend to have their characters tell them about their lives, past, present, and future. This is a really great technique, but let's take it a step further. You are going to ask your characters how they feel about everything that happens in the story.

At this point, you likely have your major plot points figured out. But, every writer has experienced the frustration that comes along when they just don't know how to move the plot forward or how to solve a plot hole that doesn't make sense. Stewing about these problems can put a giant kink in the works. It's almost impossible to move forward if these questions are hovering over you, unanswered.

Tip & Method 4 (cont.)

Here's what you can do instead-- answer these questions ahead of time. No, you can't predict every question or issue you'll have. But, you can be way ahead of the game and can be prepared to solve any issue that comes your way.

List the major plot points you have planned. Then, interview every character who will be affected or even present at the time of the event. "Ask" your characters what they saw, who they saw, what they felt, what happened (for them) before and after the major plot point. Remember to do this for each character in turn-- even minor ones. This helps you see the plot from all angles so you can plug up any holes. This can be as quick or as detailed as you want to make it.

Now, when you run into questions or aren't sure what to write next, you can just look at what your characters told you. You'll never get stuck and your writing will be even more powerful and creative.

You can also do this with non-fiction, to some extent. It depends on your topic and your goal

Tip & Method 5
Change where you are.

Writers are creatures of habit. They do the same things the same way. Sometimes, this works well-- maybe you have a lucky chair or desk you write in. Sometimes, though, this sameness causes things to go stale-- and it shows up in your writing.

If you're feeling stuck, bland, or uninspired, you need a change of scenery. Here are some ideas of things you can do to jumpstart you physically, mentally, and emotionally:

- Do something you've never done before.
- Go to the beach and brainstorm or write there.
- Go to a busy Starbucks or local cafe and write there.
- Go for a walk through the woods by yourself with no electronics.
- Take an entire week off with no access to electronics.
- People watch for an entire afternoon

Tip & Method 5 (cont.)

- Read something in a genre you've never read before
- Re-read your favorite book from childhood
- Call someone you haven't called in a while
- Apologize to someone you need to apologize to
- Pay the toll for someone behind you
- Spend the day on a farm
- Visit the "poor" section of town
- Volunteer in a homeless shelter for an afternoon
- Visit the ritzy section of town
- Dress up like someone you admire
- Read about the life of a writer from two centuries ago

… you get the idea. It's time to break out and do something completely unexpected. You may have heard this advice before, but you likely haven't seen anything like this list before. One or more of those ideas stood out to you. Now, do them.

Tip & Method 5 (cont.)

You'll come back to your writing with a new perspective, a new jolt of creativity, and total freedom to write something awesome much more quickly than you would have had you just stared at the blinking cursor for hours on end.

Tip & Method 6
Know exactly what you're doing, and when.

Do you write haphazardly? I know some writers who "write" all day long. I know some business owners who "work" all day. They'll claim to spend 16 hour days working or writing and are at their breaking point. They definitely give their blood, sweat, and tears to the craft.

If you're that type of writer or worker, I want you to look hard at what you're actually doing.

- How often do you check your email?
- How often do you visit news sites?
- How much time do you spend on Facebook?
- How often do you find yourself getting into debates on Internet forums?
- Do you check celebrity gossip sites?
- Do you find yourself getting up for a drink, to use the bathroom, to get a snack, to check on the cat dozens of times in your work day?
- Do you find yourself at the end of a work day, wondering what in the world you did all day and why you don't have more of your project done?

Tip & Method 6 (cont.)

I'll be the first to say that I work long days. But, my days are pretty tightly focused. I frequently check in on my forum members and my Facebook group members. You'll rarely find me flittering my days away doing nothing. It takes dedication to get to this point and I won't say it's always easy-- the Internet is an endlessly distracting place with any number of rabbit holes.

I want you to give yourself a maximum of 3 hours a day to work at your computer over the next three days. That's it. You're not allowed to be on your computer, for any reason, longer than three hours.

These 3 challenge hours will include the following activities:

- Writing
- Marketing your Kindle books
- Checking email
- Spending time checking news outlets, gossip, and funny cat pictures

Tip & Method 6 (cont.)

Yes, you have big projects to complete. You have goals and deadlines.

You still have those goals and deadlines...but you now have much less time to work on them for three days.

Don't worry-- I'll wager that you'll get a *lot* more done than you usually do. There are two things at work here:

- You naturally work better, faster, and more efficiently when you're crunched for time. You don't have 16 hours a day to work during this challenge, so your conscious and subconscious will find ways for you to work smarter.

- You'll neither have the time nor the inclination to check out time wasting sites. You only have 3 hours-- those dancing cats aren't *that* interesting. You also won't feel the pull to do something fun while you work so hard because you won't feel like you're missing out. You have 21 hours to do whatever else you'd like to do (assuming you don't have an outside job-- even then, your "free" hours truly become your own). Read a book, go for a walk, or watch tons of trashy TV if you want. The rest of the day belongs to you.

Tip & Method 6 (cont.)

Do a self-evaluation after the experiment. Did you get more done than normal? You probably did-- working a fraction of the time. Adjust your work day from there and think about what you have to do and what you really want to do. Those low-value time wasting websites are sucking away your productivity and time away from activities you really want to do.

Tip & Method 7
Reading is the answer.

It's impossible to become a good writer if you aren't an avid reader. There are so many amazing writers out there. Their books will change your life as you're reading.

Some writers, however, get so caught up in getting their own work out there that they neglect to feed their mind with the words of others.

Right now, you're studying a book about writing better and writing more efficiently so you can cash in more by writing amazing Kindle books. I've given you some great tips so far, but this is absolutely the most important one.

Read. Read. Read. READ.

It's amazing what happens when you read. Ideas will come to you. You'll be infinitely more creative. Words will flow easily, and in the perfect order. You'll be inspired, alive, and changed.

Tip & Method 7 (cont.)

Read fiction and nonfiction. Read spy novels, romance novels, and horror novels. Read historical fiction and nonfiction, biographies and self-help books. Read everything.

Figure out how to get Kindle books from your local library and fill your Kindle with everything you can get your hands on. That is the best writing course on the planet.

Tip & Method 8
Zippy research is within reach.

Research.

What came to mind when you read that word? How did you feel? What was your body language?

If you're like many people, you cringed. You made a face and felt a knot in your stomach. That's because so many of us are taught (and experience) that research has to be this difficult, boring, time-consuming thing.

Okay, maybe it used to be those things, but it doesn't have to be anymore. This is the best time in history to be a writer. Not only can you publish anything you want to (within reason) on Kindle, but you can access anything you need to make it happen.

You can use Google Earth to visit faraway lands. You can access untold numbers of public domain books. You can Google anything you want to know. You can ask people from all over the world

Tip & Method 8

whatever you'd like to ask them. You can find experts to interview on any topic, with a few clicks of the mouse.

Everything you need is out there and it's easily accessible. You just have to know how to find it and organize it. Sometimes, having too much information can be just as scary as not having enough.

Here are three tips you need to know to take away most of your struggle with research before you write:

1. Learn how to read only what you need to-- This is the biggest trick to research there is. Be very specific with your research and read only what you need to. Use the ctrl+f function to drill down and find specific words and sections. Be very specific with Google and database searches. Don't waste time taking notes or even reading things you don't really need to know. You aren't hoarding information-- you're reading and using only what you need.

Tip & Method 8 (cont.)

2. Organize your research as you go-- Be very specific about what you need to know. Create notes files for specific topics. Organize yourself now and you won't have to spend hours doing it later. Don't just have a giant file for a topic-- have many smaller, very specific files that you can access in a stress-free way while writing.

3. Know exactly where to get the best information-- Don't waste time using sources that can't back themselves up. Look for primary sources and scholarly sources. Use more than one source to verify information. Scholar.google.com is a great starting place as is books.google.com. Use those databases to spark additional research in the right places. Go to the right spots the first time around and you'll save yourself a lot of headaches.

Tips & Method 9
You're a character.

Writers psyche themselves out constantly. Maybe you're about to write your first book and don't even think you can call yourself a writer yet. Or, maybe you envy another writer's style and don't think you can measure up. Or, maybe you're feeling so stuck and uninspired lately that you can't complete your projects.

Whatever it is, it's time to get over it. It's zapping your creativity, output, and...your wallet.

It's time to go outside of yourself a little bit. It's time to think of yourself as a character. That might sound strange, but it really can help. Just as you would create a character sketch for someone in your books, create a character sketch for yourself as a writer. There are three steps to this:

1. Invent yourself-- Brainstorm who you are as a writer. What you look like, think about, and talk about as a writer. Now brainstorm who you ideally are as a writer. What is your process? What do people say about your work? Where do you work?

Tips & Method 9 (cont.)

2. Picture yourself-- Next, close your eyes and picture yourself writing. See yourself smiling with confidence as you type away. See yourself finishing the piece. See yourself publishing it on Kindle, happy all the while. See the praise rush in as people read the words. Get a very clear picture in mind-- create a vision board to really cement the images.

3. Interview yourself-- Finally, interview yourself. Create a list of questions you'd ask any writer you were interested in. Then, answer the questions, honestly and completely. Your answers may surprise you. They will also give you deeper insight into who you are as a writer.

This process helps you come into your own as a writer. It gives you the confidence and assurance you need to produce outstanding work, more quickly.

Tips & Method 10

The formula for writing faster than you ever have before.

Earlier, I talked about how important it is to create efficient systems in business. It's best to have a streamlined process you follow for everything you do.

It's time to create an efficient process for your writing life. This isn't meant to crush your creativity, it's to get the "what do I do next?" question out of the picture. You'll have a process for what you're doing next, leaving room for you to be more creative and better at what you do.

Here is an example narrative to help you figure out your process:

"First, I come up with story ideas. I generate story ideas by _____.

I write my story and book ideas as they come to me. Next, I choose the story I am going to work on next. When I can't decide, I

_____.

Tips & Method 10 (cont.)

This example can become anything you want it to become. The important thing is that you create a personalized system for writing. You cover your bases and leave nothing to chance. You have steps and solutions for everything. Consider this both a contract and insurance policy for yourself-- you'll never have to get off track.

Putting These 10 Tips & Methods to Use

Choose the cheats that are calling out to you. There was likely one that gave you an "ah ha!" moment.

Start by implementing that one.

Play around with the ideas, put them to use, and watch your productivity soar.

What's more is that these tips should invigorate your writing. You'll feel good about what you're doing. You'll be able to release more for Kindle than you could have dreamed before, and your readers will love it.

Putting These 10 Tips & Methods to Use (cont.)

It's all about being efficient, removing mind blocks, unleashing your potential, and letting your creativity shine through.

Don't let these ideas sit here, unused.

Writing better and faster with less work? It's a dream come true, and the gift is sitting here, waiting for you to use it.

BRINGING OUT THE POTENTIAL IN CHILDREN SERIES

- Volume 1 - Bringing Out the Potential In Children Writers/Authors
- Bringing Out the Potential In Children Writers/Authors Workbook
- Volume 2 - Bringing Out the Potential In Children Gardeners
- Bringing Out the Potential In Children Gardeners Workbook
- Volume 3 - Bringing Out the Potential In Children Cooks/Chefs
- Bringing Out the Potential In Children Cooks/Chefs Workbook

Find them at the Full Potential Store – http://fullpotential.co.place

Also find this complete series along with the **Companion Workbooks** for each of the volumes in the series **"Bringing Out The Potential In Children"** on Amazon and other fine book stores.

Other Books by Patrice Porter

The Coffee Break Author

Get past that barrier of having no time. Now we make time with "The Coffee Break Author" which breaks down the writing process into coffee break size sessions taking you step by step to the completion of your book.

Available at: http://bringoutthepotential.com

Afraid? Not Me! How I Came to Love My School and the People In It.

A children's book created by Patrice and her granddaughter, Ffion.

It's Patty's first day at school and she's a bit scared. Luckily she has Cuddles, the bunny, and her sister Ava to make her first day a wonderful day. Follow Patty's first day of school in "Afraid? Not Me! How I Came to Love My School and the People In It."

Found on Amazon and other fine book stores

Patrice Porter
Certified Educational Associate
Contact Phone - 1(306)469-5741
Website:
http://fullpotential.co.place

www.ingramcontent.com/pod-product-compliance
Lightning Source LLC
LaVergne TN
LVHW020933090426
835512LV00020B/3342